WEST *by* WATERWAY

Rivers and U.S. Expansion

WEST by WATERWAY

Rivers and U.S. Expansion

by Nicholas Nirgiotis

A First Book
Franklin Watts
New York / Chicago / London / Toronto / Sydney

Cover photographs copyright ©: The Collection of the Public Library of Cincinnati and Hamilton County; North Wind Picture Archives (inset)

Photographs copyright ©: North Wind Picture Archives: pp. 6, 11, 12, 17, 18, 21, 27, 28, 34, 38, 46, 54; Tennessee State Library and Archives: p. 14; The Bettmann Archive: pp. 20, 31, 41, 44; The Collection of the Public Library of Cincinnati and Hamilton County: pp. 25, 33, 42, 43; Archive Photos: pp. 37, 53 (American Stock); UPI/Bettmann: p. 49; De Witt Clinton High School, courtesy of Margaret Yardley Voelker: p. 50; Ohio Historical Society: p. 56.

Book Design: Herman Adler Design Group

Library of Congress Cataloging-in-Publication Data

Nirgiotis, Nicholas.
West by waterway : rivers and U.S. expansion / Nicholas Nirgiotis.
p. cm.—(A First book.)
Includes bibliographical references (p.) and index.
ISBN 0-531-20188-0
1. United States—Territorial expansion—Juvenile literature. 2. Inland navigation—United States—History—19th century—Juvenile literature. [1. United States—Territorial expansion. 2. Inland water transportation—History. 3. Frontier and pioneer life.]
I. Title. II. Series.
E179.5.N57   1995
386'.0973'09034—dc20   94-39332
                                          CIP
                                           AC

Contents

**Thus the Birch Canoe was builded
In the valley, by the river,
In the bosom of the forest;
And it floated on the river
Like a yellow leaf in Autumn,
Like a yellow water lily.**

—American poet Henry Wadsworth Longfellow, *Song of Hiawatha*

The "Mayflower" of the West

A few days before Christmas 1779, Colonel John Donelson stood on a bank of the Holston River in Virginia's western frontier to look over his fleet. Riverboats, a few rafts, and some big **dugout canoes** floated close together, like ducks in a pond. The boats were built of heavy timbers and looked ready for the long voyage ahead, but the colonel knew the dangers that awaited them.

A cold wind blew down the mountains, turning surface water to ice, and Donelson could feel his fingers stiffening. Would bad weather, he worried, prevent his small **flotilla** of riverboats from setting out? Thirty families from Virginia were placing their trust in him to lead them safely to new homes in the Cumberland Valley. Most of the Cumberland River is now part of Tennessee, but then it was a little-known place deep in America's western wilderness.

Hunters and fur traders who had ventured into this valley described it as a huge bowl sliced in the middle by a river and surrounded by ridges. The sea of tall grasses that covered the land was home to countless deer, buffalo, and elk. The soil was said to be so rich it would grow almost anything, and there were plenty of trees for building houses. For Donelson's Virginians, it was an ideal place to start

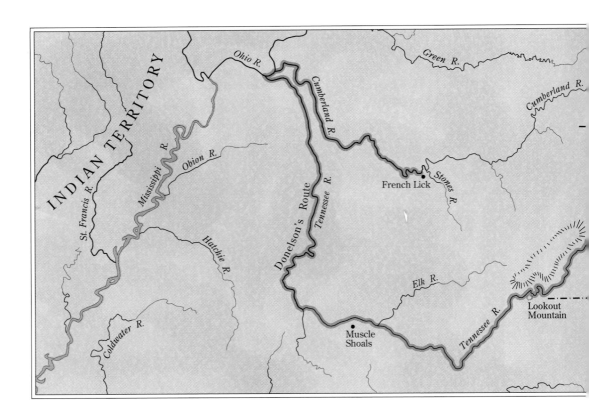

new lives. The difficulty would be getting through the thick-ly wooded and rugged Appalachian Mountains to the fertile land on the other side.

The Donelson party's leaders had found a way—they would travel to their new homes by water. Their boats and canoes would float down the Holston, a **tributary** of the Tennessee River, then down the entire 650-mile (1,046-km)

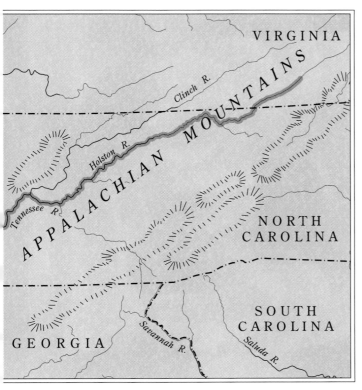

Marked in red, Donelson's route by waterway cut through the Appalachian Mountains on the Holston and Tennessee rivers, then continued up the Ohio and Cumberland rivers to French Lick.

length of the Tennessee, which flows in a southwesterly direction through the Appalachian Mountains before turning north to empty into the Ohio River. From that point the settlers would pole and paddle their boats upstream against the current, first on the Ohio, then on the Cumberland River, to their destination.

Carrying out this plan, however, would not be easy. Donelson and his group would be traveling through unknown wilderness and navigating hundred of miles of treacherous river water in winter. Before the flotilla could start its journey, the weather turned bitterly cold, and thick ice trapped the boats in their moorings until an early thaw at the end of February 1780. Finally, the group set off for the Tennessee River and Indian lands.

The year before, Virginians had raided some Cherokee towns, killing many Indians and burning their towns. The Indians responded with attacks of their own from the twisting riverbanks, which began as soon as the boats passed the first Indian towns. Although the boats were clumsy and slow, their solid shelters made of wood offered some protection. The canoes, while easier to maneuver, provided no cover and left the passengers open to attack.

When the current forced some of the boats too close to shore, the Indians killed several in Donelson's party and

When the riverways narrowed, the flatboats floated close to shore and were open to attack from Indians.

Steering the rafts safely through rapids was challenging and risky. The combination of rough water and craggy rocks crushed many a boat.

wounded many others. Near Lookout Mountain, the Indians managed to board the last boat in line. The current was too strong for any of the boats in the group to turn back and save the stranded boat. All the passengers on board were either captured or killed.

In many parts of the Tennessee River, rushing water currents and rocky riverbeds created treacherous **rapids**. Boats that hit the projecting rocks were overturned and dashed to pieces. The rest of the group rescued the wet, shivering passengers, but most of their belongings were lost. **Reefs** and sandbars could also be dangerous. When a boat ran aground, the only way out was to unload its passengers and their baggage into the shallow water and hope that the boat would float free before Indians attacked.

Worst of all were the rapids at Muscle Shoals. Donelson wrote in his diary: "When we approached the rapids they had a dreadful appearance. The water being high made a terrible roaring which could be heard at some distance. . . . Here we did not know how soon we should be dashed to pieces, and all our troubles ended at once. Our boats frequently dragged on the bottom and warped as much as in a rough sea." Luckily, due to heavy spring rains, the river was high and all the boats were able to run the rapids safely.

John Donelson and his party must have welcomed the end of
their long and trying journey and the start of new lives in
the green Tennessee mountains.

Soon in calmer waters, they floated northward 250 miles (402 km) to the Ohio without further danger. Poling and shoving the awkward, heavy boats against the current, the worn-out river travelers plodded ahead to the mouth of the Cumberland and up the river. Finally, at the end of April, they caught sight of the valley that would be their new home and the tiny settlement at French Lick, which in time grew into the city of Nashville.

It took Donelson and his party several months to travel 1,000 miles (1,609 km). They had endured bone-chilling cold, Indian attacks, hunger, fatigue, and an outbreak of smallpox. Despite the hardships, the members of Donelson's party, like the hundreds of thousands of settlers who came after, discovered that the best way to travel westward was on nature's highways—the network of rivers and lakes that threaded their way through the wilderness of forest and prairie.

2

The Beaver Men Blaze a Trail

When the first English colonists landed in North America in the early 1600s, they settled along the shores of the Atlantic. Their communities dotted the coast from Massachusetts to Virginia, and every year after that they spread westward, the way a tree adds rings to its trunk.

Those colonists, however, came up against a mighty natural barrier. The 6,000-foot- (1829-m-) high Appalachian mountain chain ran in a southwesterly direction from New England all the way to Georgia, sharply dividing the colonies on the eastern seaboard from the vast lands to the west. The densely wooded mountains stood like a wall, keeping the colonists who lived along the coastal plains from moving westward.

Shadowy forests spread unbroken over the mountainsides and, into the valleys and, as a result, the colonists feared the dark, mysterious wilderness. The lack of paths

16

The thick forests of the Appalachian Mountains were the first great barrier to westward expansion.

The early Indians of North America built canoes that were light and fast. The settlers who came afterward quickly took to this new form of transportation.

or roads wide enough for wagons made travel difficult. Only small parties could penetrate this terrain—and only then by following narrow packhorse paths or Indian trails worn deep over the centuries.

The first Europeans to cross the mountains were adventurers and explorers, and they followed the Indian trails. During their journeys, the travelers discovered an interesting fact—the trails often connected one swiftly flowing stream with another. The Indians, they learned, traveled on foot only when absolutely necessary and regularly used canoes to travel up and down the rivers in order to hunt or trade with other tribes. The Europeans quickly began to travel the same way.

An Indian canoe was the simplest of boats to build. The frame was made of cedar and spruce branches. The outside was covered with white birch bark and waterproofed with black spruce gum. The birch bark canoe was swift and graceful. It was also light enough to carry from one stream to another, an activity called **portaging.**

European explorers traveled westward in their canoes on the maze of rivers that meandered far into the interior, making notes and drawing crude maps of the land as they went. When they returned to the colonies, they told stories about all they had seen.

Their reports were glowing. The great interior valleys of the Ohio and Mississippi rivers were covered with thick woods that opened into seas of grass. So huge were these prairies that when the wind blew, the grass rippled like ocean waves. The land's fertile topsoil was so deep that in places, one could drive a sword up to the hilt without hitting a rock. The woods and prairies were the perfect home for a variety of birds, fish, and other animals. Broad rivers cut the land, and the lakes seemed to be as large as seas.

Daniel Boone captured the imaginations of Americans fascinated by the West. George Caleb Bingham, an American artist and politician, painted this picture of Daniel Boone escorting settlers through the Cumberland Gap.

The most famous American frontiersman, Daniel Boone, described the West as a "most howling wilderness," but also a rich one, watered by many rivers and full of deer, bison, wild turkey, and bear. Boone considered the sprawling woodlands a magical place where he could escape from civilization. He wandered alone or with a few companions, exploring and hunting. The West was, he said, a good place to build a home and live free of government meddling, an idea that appealed to many Americans who yearned for wide-open spaces and had the urge to move. The stories of

Boone's adventures and his descriptions of the beauty and richness of the land did much to excite interest in the West.

Although the land seemed untouched, the interior was not empty of people. Important Indian nations, including the Iroquois, the Algonquins, the Hurons, and the Cherokees, lived in this beautiful land. The Indians depended on the bountiful animal life for their existence and successfully hunted and trapped many kinds of wildlife. The colonists soon realized that they could trade European goods for animal skins with the Indians quite profitably.

Indians bring beaver skins to trade with colonists.

Traders soon followed the explorers over the mountains. Each year in the spring, they left their back-country trading posts loaded with axes, guns, blankets, mirrors, gunpowder, flints, knives, and kettles, which they traded for deerskins and beaver, bear, and otter furs to export to Europe. Beavers were an especially valuable catch. The fur was used to make expensive hats, and oil from beaver glands made up the base for perfume.

When England formally recognized the United States' independence in 1783, it also surrendered to the new nation the vast territory west of Pennsylvania between the Ohio and Mississippi rivers, known as the Northwest Territory. This enormous and valuable area added up to some 200,000,000 acres (80,937,128 ha). It would later be divided into the states of Ohio, Indiana, Michigan, Illinois, Wisconsin, and part of Minnesota.

The riches of the western lands naturally attracted settlers. Even while the War for Independence raged on, small groups began moving into the interior. When the last shots of the war had been fired, settlers pushed westward in ever-increasing numbers. Searching for the best route to their destination, these settlers found that the easiest way to travel in the wilderness was on water. The mountains may have locked them in along the coast, but the rivers would let them out.

Opening the West

Some people say "Ohio" is an Indian word that means "beautiful." Others claim the name means "great." Whatever its meaning, the Ohio River served as the main highway for opening the West. The Ohio ran 1,100 miles (1,770 km) between the clean, gentle banks of sandy but fertile soil along the southern border of the Northwest Territory. From its beginnings in Pennsylvania, it swept westward, swinging toward the south before it emptied into the Mississippi.

Not only did the Ohio flow in the right direction for the westward travelers, it was also the backbone to which the Kanawha, from West Virginia; the Muskingum and the Miami, from Ohio; the Wabash, from Indiana; and the Tennessee, from Kentucky, were joined. Then, the Ohio itself became part of a larger river network. Along with the Illinois, Wisconsin, Arkansas, Red, and Missouri rivers and many smaller streams, the Ohio River added its waters to the mighty Mississippi as it flowed on its long journey from northern Minnesota to the Gulf of Mexico.

As migration increased, numerous trails snaked their way overland from Virginia and North Carolina and South Carolina to connect with the Ohio. Settlers from New York or New England traveled by land to Warren, Pennsylvania, and then by water on the Allegheny River, which joined the Ohio River. By 1788, there were enough people at the Forks, where the Allegheny and Monongahela rivers join to form the Ohio, to lay out Pittsburgh as a town.

People moved west for many reasons. As the population of the thirteen original states increased, life became more competitive. The best land had already been taken, and many men whose older brothers would inherit their family's land went west to seek their own fortune. The generation of Americans following the War of Independence wanted to live better than their parents. They believed in progress and wanted to take advantage of the new opportunities available in the West.

Land, however, was not the only lure. Religious groups, such as the Shakers, the Mormons, Robert Owen's New Harmony Colony, and the Amana Colony found that the wide-open frontier allowed them to worship God the way they wanted. Then there were the horse thieves, gam-

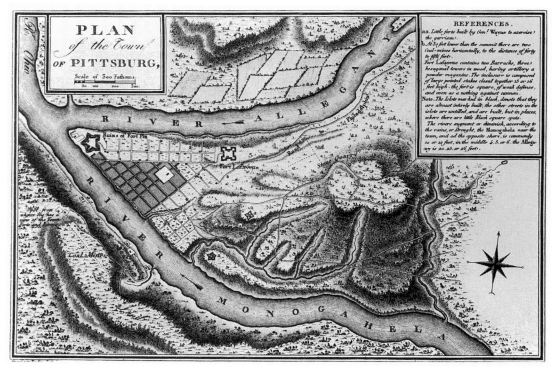

This is an early map of Pittsburgh, the town that formed near Fort Pitt at the fork of the Allegheny and Monongahela rivers. A starting point for westward travelers, Pittsburgh was called the "Gateway to the West."

blers, swindlers, and murderers who moved into the western backwoods to escape the law.

The settlers that traveled west brought along their children, their cows, pigs, horses, and chickens, and only the most essential household goods and farm tools. They came with a **warrant** for the land, either bought from land speculators or received free from the government. Congress gave land to soldiers who had fought during the Revolution, sometimes up to 1,000 acres (405 ha) if they agreed to settle in dangerous areas of the frontier. Settlers would take a piece of land, make a clearing, and build a log cabin if trees were nearby or, if on the prairies, make a house out of sod. They would plant wheat or corn for themselves and ship any extra stock back east or export it to Europe.

Although the soil was rich, the growing season long, and rainfall plentiful, backwoods life was rugged. Families were large and women and children worked alongside the men. Settlers had to work together to build homes and clear the land. Cutting down the giant trees, building the first rough cabins, plowing and planting the fields, and adding sections each season took years of hard work. Settlers' lives depended on their skills, their courage, and their willingness to share and cooperate, and they were proud of what they had accomplished.

When pioneer families settled the land, building a home was the first task, and everyone pitched in.

By 1800, on both shores of the Ohio River alone, more than thirty thousand people lived on farms and in small towns. Generally, New Englanders settled along the north bank of the river and Virginians along the south. Streams of immigrants from the eastern states moved steadily overland to Pittsburgh, where they reached the Ohio River and continued their journey westward.

Originally, the settlers' main business was farming. As the farms flourished, the farmers began to ship some of their harvest to other markets to sell and, in turn, they wanted to buy goods from the East. Some settlements quickly grew into market centers and then towns. Homes built of brick or lumber replaced the simple log cabins. The town square was marked by a courthouse and a church, which also served as the schoolhouse during the week. There was a mill, a smithy (a blacksmith's shop), and a general store. Banks, newspapers, libraries, and theaters

Like much American folk art, this illustration of Cincinnati in 1810 looks two-dimensional. Although folk artists had little or no formal training, their works have great historic and artistic value.

were added later. Such towns as Pittsburgh, Cincinnati, Louisville, and St. Louis—and later Chicago, Omaha, Cleveland, and Milwaukee—grew into great cities because of their excellent locations on rivers or lakes.

Not all the land under American control was open to settlement. Various American Indian groups owned the land on which they lived, and the U.S. government recognized that ownership. Because the groups were scattered over so wide an area, the settlers considered the land almost empty. They saw vast lands with the finest soil in the world lying unproductive, wanted to cultivate those lands, and considered the Indians living there barriers to progress.

Some settlers decided to try to buy the land from the Indians by treaty or, if that were not possible, to take the land by force. The U.S. government made several treaties with Indian nations between 1790 and 1830. The Treaty of Greenville in 1795, for example, gave the United States title to two-thirds of the state of Ohio and part of Indiana. The settlers, however, seldom kept their promises and used the treaties to evict the Indians from their homes.

One- and Two-Way Boats

When the trickle of newcomers moving westward on the rivers became a rush, they needed a bigger and more reliable boat than the canoe. Settlers began to use many different riverboats for the trip downriver. The most popular was the **flatboat**.

While some families chose to buy ready-made flatboats, more often several families would join together to build a boat from trees they cut down on the spot. Loaded with entire families, animals, supplies for the trip, farm tools, and household goods, the newly built flatboats then floated westward with the current.

Flatboats varied in size, depending on the needs of the passengers, but generally they were from 20 to 40 feet (6 to 12 m) long and 10 feet (3 m) wide. They were made of big, square timbers and their hulls rose 3 to 4 feet (1 to 1.2 m) above the water level. A structure much like a log cabin ran almost the entire length of the boat.

After crossing the Appalachian Mountains, pioneers travel on a flatboat with their livestock down the Ohio River.

Flatboats depended heavily on the river current to float them downstream. They had a couple of oars on each side to steady the boat and one long sweep at the back end to steer. Because the flatboats were able to travel only in a downstream direction, they were called one-way boats.

The settlers also depended on some luck to guide them safely along the rivers. If the water was low, rocks and sandbars could easily wreck a boat. The trunks of uprooted trees caught on the river bottom, or **snags**, sometimes speared boats and completely destroyed them. River pirates, known to kill all on board, were also a concern. The most notorious pirates had their hideout in a cave, known as Cave-in-Rock, near Shawneetown, Illinois. Settlers passed though Cave-in-Rock with great caution and tried to travel in groups whenever possible.

Once a flatboat reached its destination along the Ohio or the Mississippi, the settlers would break it down into lumber to build a cabin in a forest clearing. If a merchant had built the boat, the cargo was sold first, and then the lumber.

In time, the settlers wanted to be able to travel upstream as well as downstream, and so they designed the **keelboat**. This boat had a pointed bow (the front end) and a pointed stern (the back end) as well as a keel (a timber or metal piece running down the center of the bottom of

The contoured keelboat cut through the water more efficiently than the boxy flatboat. Sails also helped to speed the vessel along.

the boat). The keel gave stability to the frame of the boat and made it move more easily in the water. Because of its design, a keelboat could glide in the water faster than a flatboat.

The keelboat was long and narrow, 40 to 70 feet (12 to 21 m) long and 9 feet (2.7 m) wide. The body was enclosed and roofed with planks, and the main cabin was divided into rooms. Sometimes a keelboat carried a mast with sails and was large enough to carry 20 to 40 tons (18,000 to 36,000 kg) of freight. This kind of keelboat was

When the water was rough or shallow, a crew had to pull their boat with a towrope, called a cordelle.

expensive to build, however, so only wealthy merchants could afford them.

Moving the boat upstream and against the river current required human strength. Keelboatmen, facing the stern of the boat, would push 12-foot- (3.6-m-) long, iron-tipped poles against the bottom of the river as they walked from the bow toward the stern on the boat's running board. When each keeler reached the stern, he took his pole out of the water, returned to the bow, and started the work all over again. To steer the boat, the captain used a rudder. If the current were very strong, the crew had to walk along the shore and pull the boat with a towline, a process called **cordelling**. The current could carry a boat 5 miles (8 km) an hour downstream. Muscle power would push it upstream 1 mile (1.6 km) an hour.

Because keelboats could go from the large rivers into smaller streams, they helped smaller settlements in the back country keep in touch with each other and with the towns that were sprouting up along the rivers. Unfortunately, the boats were still slow. A round-trip from Pittsburgh to New Orleans could take six months—six weeks down and four and a half months back. Cincinnati to Pittsburgh was a twelve-day trip.

The keelboatmen who made these long trips were tough and hardy. In the early days, pirates and hostile Indians, whose vast hunting grounds bordered the water, made traveling the rivers dangerous. The boatmen had to be good fighters as well as skilled enough sailors to keep their boats from being wrecked or overturned in rough water. And they had to be strong to pole or pull their heavy boats upstream, often working from sunup to sundown without rest.

Although the keelboatmen worked hard, they also made the most of the river life, playing pranks, telling tales, and singing. One of their songs boasts:

> *The boatman is a lucky man,*
> *No one can dance as the boatman can;*
> *The boatmen dance and the boatmen sing,*
> *The boatman is up to anything.*
> *Hi-O away we go,*
> *Floating down the river*
> *On the O-hi-o.*
> *When the boatman goes on shore,*
> *All men run when they hear him roar.*

One legendary keelboater was Mike Fink, "the king of the keelers" on the Ohio River. He boasted that he was half horse and half alligator, and his nickname was "Snapping Turtle." Mike was a powerful man and a brawler who would challenge almost anyone to a fight. He bragged that unless he fought regularly, he would get rusty.

Another well-known American frontiersman, hunter, and scout, David Crockett, was a keelboatman for several years before he entered politics. Henry Miller Shreve, who

TELFER CINCINNATI.

One of Mike Fink's famous feats was to place a tin cup filled with whiskey on someone's head and shoot at it with a rifle. It was said the cup was always bored through without injury to anyone.

later designed and captained the first **steamboat** to sail from New Orleans to Pittsburgh, got his experience with the river as a keeler. Even future sixteenth president Abraham Lincoln had contact with keelers on two flatboat trips he made to New Orleans.

In 1803, the United States bought the **Louisiana Purchase** from France in a deal that included all the land

The Lewis and Clark expedition left from a camp near St. Louis in 1804 and reached the Pacific Ocean a year later. On the trip home, the party split into two groups to travel down the Mississippi and Yellowstone rivers and returned to St. Louis in 1806.

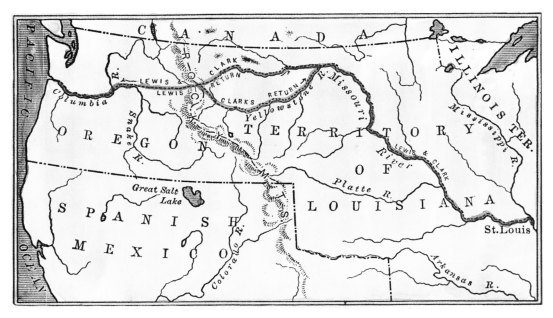

that was not controlled by Spain west of the Mississippi to the Pacific Ocean. As soon as the sale was completed, President Thomas Jefferson sent two former army officers, Meriwether Lewis and William Clark, on an expedition to explore and map America's newest possession.

The group sailed in a large keelboat up the Missouri River. They battled their way against the current, constantly on their guard against Indian attack; spent a long winter in Dakota territory suffering from extreme cold; and from there continued in canoes across present-day Montana. They then traversed the Rocky Mountains to the Clearwater and Snake rivers and sailed to the mouth of the mighty Columbia, where they had their first view of the Pacific Ocean. Traveling mainly by water, the Lewis and Clark expedition had linked the territories of the young country from coast to coast and opened the gates for the great flood of settlers moving west.

About the time of the Lewis and Clark expedition, a new boat powered by steam was developed and the number of clumsy, slow-moving flatboats and keelboats declined. By the mid-1800s, the one- and two-way boats, which had carried so many pioneer families west to farm the land, raise cattle in the vast plains, and develop the mining wealth of the region, disappeared completely.

Here Come the Fire Canoes

Even before keelboat traffic had reached its peak, an American inventor and engineer named Robert Fulton designed a boat driven by steam that could paddle as easily upstream, against the current, as downstream. In 1807, Fulton's steamboat *Clermont* successfully navigated the Hudson River from New York City to Albany. The journey marked the beginning of speedy, two-way transportation on the network of western rivers.

Within four years, the steamboat *New Orleans* made its trial run from Pittsburgh, where it had been built, to New Orleans. The strange steamboat created a stir all along the Ohio, and townspeople lined the riverbanks to admire it. Huge paddles on a large, slow-turning stern wheel splashed in the water as they pushed the boat forward. Propelled by fire and machines, it had no need for sails, poles, or backbreaking human labor. Indians who came to see the new boat gazed with amazement at the

Robert Fulton's steamboat *Clermont* carried passengers from New York City to Albany in about thirty hours, a fraction of the time a sailboat took.

tall pipe on its deck—a pipe that spit a cloud of dense smoke mixed with fiery sparks into the sky—and dubbed the boat the "fire canoe."

On the return trip, however, the *New Orleans* was unable to fight the strong Mississippi currents past the city of Natchez. The first steamboat to complete the trip from New Orleans to Pittsburgh was Henry Miller Shreve's powerful *Enterprise*, in 1815. With the success of the *Enterprise*, the steamboat era had begun in earnest, and the business of transporting passengers and goods by water was booming and profitable.

The first steamboats were small and had one deck. Their engines were deep inside the hull (or frame) of the ship, which made it difficult to navigate in low water. Later, the engines were placed on the deck. The flat hulls were shallower, and the boat could float in just 4 feet (1.2 m) of water. As the steamboats increased in size, they gained decks, allowing them to carry 1,000 tons (907,000 kg) of freight and hundreds of passengers.

Steamboats such as the *Paragon* revolutionized travel to and from the West.

During their time, steamboats were finer than anything afloat. The stacked white decks made the ships look like wedding cakes. Passengers felt they were on a floating luxury hotel, with fine cabins, stained glass windows, furniture made of rich woods, and elegant dining rooms with crystal chandeliers. Mark Twain described the romance of steamboat life in his book *Life on the Mississippi*.

By 1832, there were nearly five hundred steamboats puffing up and down the western rivers. In 1835, the number had grown to nearly seven hundred, and in 1846 to twelve hundred. Most were built in Pittsburgh, Cincinnati, or Louisville. Loaded with manufactured goods from the East, the steamboats helped commerce to flourish. The boats also delivered settlers by the thousands to their destinations in days instead of weeks or months.

In the rivalry to build newer and faster steamboats, safety was sometimes overlooked. Here, a steamboat engine blows into the sky.

Steamboats had one major drawback. Their flimsy design made them dangerous. The high-pressure boilers that powered the boat would sometimes explode, killing hundreds of people. In one of the worst tragedies, the steamboat *Moselle* blew up near Cincinnati in 1838, killing nearly 200 passengers and injuring many more. When another boat, *Orinoko*, exploded, 120 people died. To improve safety conditions, the government ordered improvements in the design of boilers. Despite many accidents, steamboat traffic continued to expand, helping the rapid development of the West and the unification of the country.

At first, steamboats provided regular service on the Ohio and lower Mississippi rivers. Later, they expanded into the upper Mississippi, the Missouri, the Tennessee, the Arkansas, and the Yellowstone. A steamboat first navigated the Missouri in 1819 and the upper Mississippi in 1823. Although the Missouri was one of the wildest rivers in North America, it had become a principal water highway by the mid-1800s. The river's violent currents, frequent snags, and sandbars in the mountainous areas made it hard to navigate. Eventually, the shallow draft boats overcame these problems, and migration into the upper Missouri and Yellowstone valleys grew even more. As towns sprang up, more goods needed to be shipped, and so more steamboats came into service.

In time, the steamboats were introduced into the Sacramento and Columbia rivers on the West Coast. Even when railroads began to compete with them for passenger traffic after the Civil War, steamboats continued to carry freight until the early 1900s.

Workers load cattle and corn onto a steamboat on the Mississippi River.

Man-made
Waterways

By 1810, more than one million people had settled in the western territories. Their farms generated bountiful crops of wheat, corn, barley, and rye. Sawmills, built along the rivers, turned trees to lumber for sale in Pittsburgh or New Orleans. Western flour, whiskey, cider, leather, furniture, beef, pork, wool, and salt were in demand in the East. With no wagon roads over the mountains, however, transporting the goods took great effort. Packhorses had to carry these western products from Pittsburgh and other river towns to markets in Philadelphia, Baltimore, and New York, a system that was slow and expensive. It was agreed that the way to improve trade and the movement of people across the United States was to build a **canal** that would connect the waterways in the interior with those in the East.

The solution for the best route for a canal through the Appalachians lay in upstate New York. Over many thousands of years, the Mohawk River had cut a valley across the mountains as it flowed eastward into the Hudson River near Albany. The pass was narrow and rough, but it was the only water-level opening through the mountains. Although the river was not **navigable**, the pass was ideal for building a canal. Once over the mountains, the way was open to the wide waters of Lake Erie, on the northern edge of the Northwest Territory.

The citizens of New York City, however, were unhappy about paying taxes for a canal that would benefit primarily the northern part of the state and opposed the projected waterway. Fortunately, the governor of New York at that time, De Witt Clinton, was convinced that canal traffic would ultimately help New York City become richer and more powerful and used his political influence to promote construction of the canal. Work began on July 4, 1817.

At that time, the Erie Canal was the largest public work ever attempted by the new country. Crews had to dig long channels through high ground with primitive tools, fill in low areas, and cut through the huge Montezuma Swampland near Syracuse. Muddy soil and a fever transmitted by mosquitoes, which killed many workers, made this section particularly difficult to complete. Because the canal was 565 feet (172 m) higher at Lake Erie than at the Hudson River, eighty-three **locks** were needed to help raise or

The Erie Canal took a tremendous amount of work to finish. Even after the canal opened, workers kept busy repairing and widening it.

To celebrate the completion of the Erie Canal, Governor
De Witt Clinton (standing far right) led a procession of boats
down the canal from Buffalo to New York.

lower boats to the next level of water. At Lockport, near Buffalo, a double set of five locks allowed canal boats to climb up or down the side of a cliff.

Although none of the builders were professional engineers, they were inventive. Where rivers had to be crossed, they built water-carrying bridges, called **aqueducts**, that were supported by arches. The aqueduct over the Genesee River near Rochester was the longest arch bridge made of stone in the world at that time. And when they hit solid rock, they used black powder to blast their way.

Whenever necessary, the workers built bridges across the canal for farmers and others to cross over the water. The bridges, however, were built low to save money. Passengers sightseeing on the decks of the canal boats had to bend down to avoid being hit on the head. "Low bridge, everybody down" was a command frequently heard near the bridges.

The 363-mile (584-km) canal was finally finished on October 26, 1825. It measured 40 feet (12 m) wide and 4 feet (1.2 m) deep. A grand procession of boats carrying Governor Clinton and other dignitaries started at Buffalo and proceeded to New York harbor to celebrate the canal's opening. At the "Wedding of the Waters" ceremony in New York harbor, a cask of Erie water was emptied into the

Atlantic Ocean to mark the completion of the canal and the joining of the East Coast to the new lands in the West.

Hundreds of canal boats from passenger packets to freight boats kept the canal busy from early spring to late fall, when the water froze. Horses or mules walked a tow-path alongside the canal, towing the boats. The legal speed limit was 4 miles (6.4 km) per hour.

The population along the canal route increased rapidly. Schenectady, Rochester, Syracuse, Buffalo, and other communities increased fivefold, and farms filled the country between them. The states bordering the Great Lakes also developed rapidly. Canal boats brought Yankees from the eastern states and immigrants from Ireland, England, Germany, Italy, and the Scandinavian countries to Buffalo, where they were crowded aboard steamboats, along with all their possessions, and carried to ports farther west.

Growing traffic spread prosperity to the communities the canal served and beyond. The Erie Canal was now the main highway for many thousands of merchants and traders who traveled back and forth on business. The Erie Canal was so heavily traveled, it became the principal East-West "street" of the nation.

New settlers poured through the canal into the prairies and turned the fields into seas of wheat and corn.

Floating on a canalboat down the Erie Canal was often much less work than covering the same distance by wagon.

By the mid-1850s, Chicago was shipping more grain than any other port in the world. The ships carried wheat and other produce on their return eastward through the Erie Canal to the East Coast. Ship traffic was heavy on the Great Lakes. Almost one thousand steamers stopped in Cleveland in 1836.

The country's westernmost canal connected Lake Michigan with the Illinois River. Here, vessels carrying grain follow a towboat out of Chicago to that canal.

The mass migration helped Detroit, Cleveland, Toledo, Chicago, and Milwaukee grow into great industrial centers. The canal put nearly fifty thousand people to work, operating the boats, the locks, and the other services. The fleet of canal boats grew from three thousand in 1836 to seven thousand by the end of the Civil War in 1865.

Even before the Erie Canal was completed, people in other states wanted their own canals. Pennsylvania, Massachusetts, New Jersey, Virginia, Ohio, Indiana, Michigan, and Illinois began building canals, many going north-south to join the Great Lakes with the Ohio. A network of 4,000 miles (6,400 km) of canals connected rivers with lakes and with each other, but none was as successful as the "Big Ditch," as the Erie Canal was nicknamed.

The Chesapeake and Ohio Canal, first proposed by George Washington, attempted to connect the Potomac River with the Ohio by cutting through the mountains west of Washington, D.C. Many long stretches of rock and the need for aqueducts slowed progess. In 1850, 185 miles (298 km) of the waterway were finally completed.

At about the same time, a network of iron rails had begun to cover the country, competing with the waterways for passengers and cargo. The railroads could go to more places, faster and more comfortably, than the riverboats. Slowly, the railroads took the passenger traffic away from the riverboats and a good deal of the freight as well.

Just as use of the keelboat overtook that of the flatboat, in time the steam train replaced the steamboat.

Between 1790 and 1850 the population of the United States increased fivefold. Attracted by cheap land and wide open spaces, a great number of Americans moved west. The rivers, lakes, and canals were the great highways over which they traveled into the interior to turn its forests and prairies into prosperous farms and thriving towns. People naturally clustered along the waterways, which became the commercial lifelines of the growing area. Gradually, some of the small towns that had sprouted at strategic spots along the waterways grew into great cities, teeming with people from many backgrounds.

Arkansas, Illinois, Indiana, Iowa, Kansas, Kentucky, Louisiana, Michigan, Minnesota, Mississippi, Ohio, Tennessee, and Wisconsin gained their early populations because of the inland waterways. Settlement of the Northwest Territory and the Mississippi Valley was only the earliest stage of the movement west. The process was repeated west of the Mississippi, first into the Louisiana Purchase, then into the Rocky Mountains, and finally to the shores of the Pacific Ocean. The settling of the West by waterway was a great adventure that absorbed the energies of Americans from the time of the first canoe trips to the turn of the century.

Glossary

Aqueduct—A structure much like a bridge, with a water channel instead of a road. Used to transport boats over a river or to bring water to a city.

Canal—A man-made waterway for boats.

Cordelling—Pulling a keelboat upriver with a rope called a cordelle.

Dugout canoe—A heavy but unsinkable canoe made of a large, hollowed-out tree trunk. The bow is rounded and the bottom is usually flat.

Flatboat—A large, flat-bottomed boat made of heavy timber for use in rivers. Flatboats can drift only downstream, with the current.

Flotilla—A fleet of small boats.

Keelboat—A large wooden riverboat built on a keel. It is poled or towed and often has a mast with sails.

Lock—An enclosed space in a canal or river with gates at either end. The water level in a lock changes to lower or raise a boat.

Louisiana Purchase—A large region extending west of the Mississippi River to the Rocky Mountains and from Canada to the Gulf of Mexico. The United States purchased this region from France in 1803 for $15 million.

Navigable—Deep and wide enough to allow boats to pass.

Portaging—Carrying a canoe and its cargo across land from one stream to another.

Rapids—The part of a river where the current flows very fast, usually over rocks.

Reef—A ridge or sandbar at or below the surface of the water.

Snag—An uprooted tree held fast in an upright position on the bottom of the river. The branches just below the surface of the water can gash the hull of any boats that pass over it.

Steamboat—A boat that is driven by steam and used on rivers and lakes.

Tributary—A river that flows into a bigger river or another body of water.

Warrant—A written order giving someone the right to do or buy something, such as a piece of land.

For Further Reading

Ault, Phil. *Whistles Round the Bend.* New York: Dodd Mead and Co., 1982.

Blumberg, Rhoda. *The Incredible Journey of Lewis and Clark.* New York: Lothrop, 1987.

Cavan, Seamus. *Daniel Boone and the Opening of the Ohio Country.* New York: Chelsea House, 1991.

Duke, Donald. *Water Trails West.* New York: Doubleday and Co., 1978.

McCall, Edith. *Pioneers on Early Waterways.* Chicago: Childrens Press, 1980.

_____. *Steamboats to the West.* Chicago: Childrens Press, 1980.

Nirgiotis, Nicholas. *Erie Canal: Gateway to the West.* New York: Franklin Watts, 1993.

Index

About the Author

Nicholas Nirgiotis was born in Chicago, where he has lived most of his life. He is a graduate of the University of Chicago and has been a teacher and freelance writer. He also wrote the Watts First Book *Erie Canal: Gateway to the West*. Mr. Nirgiotis is married and has two children.